ROADMAP TO YOUR SOUL'S CALLING

ESSENTIAL EXERCISES TO HELP YOU DISCOVER WHY YOU CAME HERE

Bev Barnes

ISBN: 978-1-4834-6436-7 (sc)
ISBN: 978-1-4834-6435-0 (e)

Lulu Publishing Services rev. date: 3/8/2017

This book is for the younger version of me, when I didn't know who I was and what I was here to do but I wanted to know. I knew there was something I was born for, but I couldn't find it, and I didn't even know how to search.

My hope is that this book will guide you and be your roadmap. I know for certain there is a way out AND that you have a purpose that is waiting for you.

To Luc and Zachary,
Thank you so much for listening to me when I became a coaching-nerd and letting me fully engage in this passionate purpose of mine. Thank you for helping me to not take myself so seriously. I'll always be your Master Spiral Burger.

My overwhelming thanks also to Jocelyn Ring who brought my Roadmap to life with her magical and intuitive visual facilitation skills. This book would not have been written had Jocelyn not brought the Roadmap out of my heart and onto the page.

ABOUT THE AUTHOR

Bev Barnes is a Soul's Purpose Mentor, Master Life & Business Coach and an expert facilitator and teacher. She believes the world is undergoing a massive transformation right now, shifting from being ego-led to being soul-led, and that many of us who have been hiding are being called to rise up and lead this *Soul Revolution*.

Bev's calling is to help the healers, guides, teachers and leaders of the Soul Revolution to rise up, own their genius and do what they came here to earth to do. She helps her clients remember their soul's purpose and get through fear and doubt so they can create a business that answers their soul's calling.

She holds a Master's degree in Psycho-Education, a graduate diploma in Brief and Strategic Therapy, has trained as a Career Counselor and is a certified Master Life Coach.

> *"Intuitive, Insightful, and endlessly supportive, Bev Barnes is the kind of coach who can help you back up and see the entire 'forest' of your life, then zero in and find your way through the trees. Because she pays such close attention to every client, she helps them see themselves more clearly, in ways that lead naturally to the understanding and fulfillment of their individual destinies."*
>
> **Martha Beck PhD, author and monthly columnist for O, The Oprah Magazine**

Bev is the creator of the **Soul's Calling Roadmap**, the **Soul's Calling Coach Training** and the **See Your Soul Self Retreat & Soul Sistah Master-Mind**.

Find out more at www.bevbarnes.com

CONTENTS

PREFACE

We all ache to be really seen, to be valued for who we are without self-improvement. We all ache to do something meaningful with our lives, something that makes a difference, but we are taught from a very young age to ignore those yearnings and fit into society. We hide who we really are and pretend to be who we are expected to be. That leads to a soul-felt angst and divine discontent.

That is how your soul calls you. Your soul is trying to wake you up to who you really are so you'll start being the person you were born to be. That's also how you find purpose and meaning, by being the real you in all aspects of your life. When you do that, your life clicks into place, and it starts to feel "right", not "wrong".

I wrote this book because I've been a lifelong purpose-seeker and I always wanted a guide. This book is your guide.

At four years old, I questioned why we were here on earth. I couldn't find an answer, and no one else was asking the question, so I hid the question inside me and did what everyone else did – school, university, a relationship, a job. That's when my soul started to ache. Something was missing, but I didn't know what it was. I was miserable in my job and my relationship. I looked for guidance in books, but there was very little in the late 1980s and early 1990s, so I made up my own process to find purpose and meaning – and it worked!

I discovered that my purpose was to facilitate renewal by helping people to see their own beauty – their unique genius and soul's purpose. How ironic.

I'm writing this book now, because the transformation of consciousness from ego to soul, written about in spiritual literature for at least 30 years, is no longer something that is coming in the future, it's happening now.

The world is struggling to shift from being ego-led to soul-led. For many, many years the ego has been in charge. That has meant that many of our society's values have been based around the goal of acquiring wealth, an ego-based goal. For the soul, nothing is wrong with wealth, but it's a by-product, not a goal. The soul knows that the only thing that's real is love and that our only goal is to enhance and increase love on the planet. Everything else is an illusion.

The soul of the world has had enough. Things are erupting. An epic battle is underway between the soul and the ego. We have the opportunity now to shape and transform the world if we each do our own individual work and shift from ego to soul in our own lives. That's why I've written this book now; to give you a roadmap to help you hear and answer *your* soul calling. If enough of us do our own work, we'll reach a tipping point, and this transformation of consciousness will occur.

Here's what you need to know right now:

1. **If you hear the call, then you have a role to play in the Soul Revolution.**

   If you have often felt angst and discontent, if you have constantly been seeking meaning and purpose, then you were born to help the world make this transformation from ego to soul. You'll find what your role is by making a commitment to discovering it.

2. **Even if you don't know what your passions are or what your purpose is, you have both.**

   This book was written primarily for people who don't know what they are passionate about and have no idea what their purpose is. This book will help you figure out what you want.

3. **Don't limit your search for meaning to a search for a "dream" job or career.**

   This book is about creating a life, not finding a dream job. Your calling might not be paid work. You might be called to create a business or a movement. Allow yourself to be open to all possibilities.

4. **You'll need to constantly re-create and reinvent your life and work as you change and grow.**

   There is no one "job" that is made for you. You can't rely on luck to end up in a life you love. We aren't taught in school how to create our own lives, so this is a new skill for you to learn. It's an active process rather than a passive one. That's why this book includes step-by-step exercises, activities and a roadmap to guide you.

5. **Shifting from a life where you feel trapped to one where you feel freedom and find meaning is a process of transformation.**

   This is not just a process of discovering what you do well or what you love that you never recognized or acknowledged, it is a process of unraveling or unlearning the rules you've lived by that led you towards ego-based goals rather than soul-based ones. This book includes exercises to help you deal with the difficult emotions of transition as well as how to find your passions and purpose.

6. **You might be a soul-inspired entrepreneur.**

   Soul-inspired entrepreneurs are those who create a business because the best way to answer their soul's calling is to create their work. They are a new breed of entrepreneur, motivated by using their gifts to meet the world's needs, rather than being motivated by profit or by being in business. In fact many soul-inspired entrepreneurs never dreamed they'd be in business. Making a living is important, but financial profit is a result of their work, not the goal.

This book is designed as your roadmap, to give you a place to explore, exercises to do and actions to take. I wanted this book to be like having me as your personal coach, mentor, challenger and supporter as you dare to decide to hear and answer your soul's calling.

Welcome!

INTRODUCTION

Have you ever wondered what it would be like to know, without a shadow of a doubt, that you were doing what you came here to do? Imagine claiming your unique purpose and fulfilling that in the most joyful way possible. If you've ever lied to yourself about being satisfied with your life or pretended to like a job you hated because you felt trapped, don't despair. You came here for a reason. When you find that reason and start living it, you'll find your freedom.

I promise you that.

I wrote this book to help you understand how to hear your soul's calling and give you practical exercises and practices that will teach you what you don't learn in school – how to figure out what you came here for.

If you are questioning your purpose now, then you came here to do something that the world needs and your soul is urging you to do it.

So many people are frustrated with what's happening in the world – the Brexit vote in Europe, the election of Donald Trump as president of the United States, the rise of the far-right wing in France. It feels like the world is in a huge period of denial: denial that the population has shifted and now includes women and people of colour; denial that the climate has changed, that the planet is heating up, and this has dire consequences for our survival; denial that the patriarchal system has run its course; denial that the gap between the "haves" and the "have-nots" is cavernous; denial that no one person or institution or country is going to save us from ourselves.

The denial is fear of change. The world has changed. We can't go back and pretend that it hasn't. Many of us were marginalized in that old world, so for us, the "good old days" weren't so good.

Some of us aren't in denial.

We feel confusion, sadness and anger. We feel the chaos. We feel a call to do something, to bring goodness and kindness and love to the world. The call feels urgent. If you are hearing or feeling this call, you are probably someone who came here to do something.

You came here with a purpose, and my guess is you came here to facilitate the transformation of consciousness in the world – from an ego-based consciousness, led by fear to a soul-based consciousness, led by love.

This is what I call the *Soul Revolution.*

It's here. It's now. It's time.

If this resonates for you deep in your bones, then you have a role to play. That role doesn't have to be big. Your role is to do the one small task you do best that gives you the most joy. That's what'll help the world shift to a soul-based consciousness. Start with your own life first. You'll need to transform yourself before you can transform the world.

Your real life begins when you dare to decide to hear and answer your soul's calling.

There is a reason you are here. Your soul knows that reason and tries to guide you through your whole life, but you haven't learned your soul's language yet.

In this book you'll learn the language of your soul and start listening to her, developing a relationship of trust with her and following her guidance. Learning your soul's language will change your life. It will lead you to the gut-level knowing that you are doing what you were made for and you'll go from feeling lost to being found. You'll find a deep inner satisfaction that you are being who you were born to be.

The exercises in this book teach you the language of the soul and guide you through the Soul's Calling Roadmap – a metaphor and visual map for the journey that people take when transforming their lives and work from leading with their ego to leading with their soul.

How do I know all this?

I've been exactly where you are now, and I figured out how to renew and transform my own life. Here's a bit of my story—

When I was growing up, I followed all the rules. I was a good student and a good, kind person. I was from an immigrant family and one of very few black people in the school, and I tried hard to fit in and not be noticed. I believed my job in life was to assimilate. There were very few people of colour in Canada when I was growing up. I thought if I fit in I'd be safe from criticism and discrimination. I was deathly afraid of being rejected. Highly empathic, it was easy for me to figure out the rules and follow them – which is exactly what I did.

By the time I was 30 years old, I had a life that looked good on the outside, but it was totally unfulfilling on the inside. When you are busy following everyone else's rules and trying to blend in, you stop seeing yourself. You stop hearing the whispers of your soul trying to guide you. You lose the inner compass of desire because you've all but shut that down. You end up knowing what you don't like but not knowing what you want or what you do like.

I had a good job with lots of responsibilities, a great salary and regular business travel. I rewarded myself with a cute downtown apartment with a real fireplace, stylish clothes and a nice car. I was living the single-girl life I'd envisioned. I was Mary from the *Mary Tyler Moore Show*, who I'd grown up watching on television.

But every night after work I'd go home totally wiped out, exhausted with absolutely no energy. I thought something was wrong with that. Did other people crash on the couch every night after work? How could that be normal for someone my age? I was bored and frustrated. While my government job had a noble cause, I wasn't interested in it at all.

I kept my boredom and frustration to myself. I pretended all was well. I was competent and well-respected on the outside, but I felt like I was dying on the inside. I remember the day I was told I was now "permanent" in my job. I felt a pit in the bottom of my stomach. All it meant to me was I would get another week of vacation in seven years. I wanted to run screaming into the night. I felt like I was putting my soul in prison.

Most women escape into their relationships or their children when they are miserable at work. I couldn't because I was single and my long-term relationship was going nowhere fast. I was ignoring the obvious: both my job and my relationship were wrong for me. I was in deep denial.

My shape-shifting habit – being what other people wanted me to be – had caused me to totally lose myself. Whose life was this anyway? It sure didn't feel like mine. I knew I wasn't born to be a senior manager in a government organization, but I didn't know who I was. I felt SO trapped. I was totally lost and miserable, pretending to be fine but drowning under the weight of a divine discontent and bone-deep angst.

Can you relate?

Divine discontent is your soul calling.

The soul calls in different ways. It starts with whispers, a slow burn, the gradual onset of a low-level malaise that won't go away. If you don't listen to the whispers, then you get a nudge. There's a collapse: a job loss, a painful divorce, an illness, the death of someone close. The soul, I believe, is orchestrating your life to help you learn the lessons you need to learn so you can do what you came here for. But it's not always pleasant; it's often painful. It feels like an erupting volcano. The soul does what it must for you to hear her call.

Your soul is calling you to do what you came for. And you came here for a reason.

Your soul wants you to stop leading your life with your ego or the way you were socialized to please and pretend, and start leading your life with *her* – your unflinching truth. Things start to fall apart in your life to wake you up and nudge you to make changes, so you start living your "real" life rather than the "fake" one that doesn't fit.

I call the falling apart process *the erupting volcano.*

Everyone who makes a major life shift has a volcano erupt in their life that can't be ignored. A door closes – something you wanted is irrevocably lost – and you must dare to decide to go in a different direction than you thought you would.

Michael Meade, renowned storyteller, author and scholar, calls this *the second birth.* He says:

> *The second birth involves the uncovering and discovering of the genius nature of the individual soul. The second birth is an inner event; a psychological birth intended to awaken each of us to the original agreement of our souls.*

My volcano erupted when I was downsized and lost my job, discovered I was pregnant and my relationship ended all at the same time.

This book is based on the steps I took to renew and transform my life. I've worked with thousands of people over the past twenty years to do the same thing. I created an acronym – S.O.U.L. – to help you easily remember the steps.

S – Stopped the Denial.

I admitted I was miserable in all aspects of my life. I can cope with much misery for far longer than most people. I first had to admit to myself that I was miserable. Even without making any changes, I needed to stop shoving down my emotions and denying my truth. I had to recognize my volcano was erupting and it was time to make a decision to change something.

I dared to decide. I made a *No Matter What* decision. I decided to believe I had a purpose. I decided to stop being a victim and take responsibility for my life. I decided I was capable of changing. I couldn't be the only person who didn't have a purpose, could I? I decided I was going to find something I loved, something that was made for me to do – NO MATTER WHAT.

I focused on work because it was easier for me to think about making changes in my work than making changes in my relationship. I decided that if I became congruent in one area of my life, it would spill over into all areas of my life and my relationship would either get better or end. This proved to be true.

O – Outed My Truth.

I started a daily meditation practice. I was so used to pretending I was fine, pretending I agreed with other people, that I didn't know my own truth or how to find it. I took a meditation course because a psychic I'd seen suggested the answers lay inside me. That led to three years of daily meditation. I'm not saying you have to meditate daily for three years, but you need to get familiar with the quiet, deep inner part of you that is beyond your verbal mind. When you do that, you know what your truth is, because you know how it feels in your body. Your soul speaks to you through your body.

I committed to congruence. I made the intention to be the same person on the outside as I was on the inside in all aspects of my life. I didn't have to *do* anything; I just had to start living my truth. This is easy to say but not so easy to do. You can't pretend you like doing things you hate, and you need to start saying *No* to others so you can say *Yes* to yourself.

I stopped unconsciously following other people's rules and consciously chose my own. This rolled out naturally from my decision to be congruent. I couldn't live my truth if I was busy intuiting what people wanted me to be and trying to be that. I couldn't live my truth if I was following cultural norms or gender roles or all the other unconscious rules we follow in our lives without ever examining if they are our deepest truth.

U – Unlocked My Genius.

I got clear on my own genius and started to OWN it! I had no idea that I had gifts. All I knew was I was an alien in my workplace. I had an idea I was different than the people I worked with, but I didn't value that difference. I needed to find and claim who I was with no apologies. I needed to be able to name and own my spectacular gift of empathy and my ability to connect with people. I needed to realize these gifts were given to me to help me fulfill my soul's purpose, which was etched inside my life. Finding my own genius was a deep dive inside to excavate the gems I had been ignoring.

L – Lead with Love Not Fear

I started to follow *only* joy. I was bored, exhausted and probably slightly depressed when I started this journey. I had no passions to speak of. I had no deep desires and so I thought something was wrong with me or that I was just one of those people who didn't have any passions. I went on a voyage of discovery to uncover what made me light up. I started tracking my joy.

I felt afraid and took action anyway. I became a doer. Once I had a thread of joy, I tried things out; I took courses, initiated projects, made connections. I started a group in my home of people I didn't know that well. We called ourselves *The Dream Team,* and I facilitated that self-discovery group for three years. That group was a clear signpost to my passions my purpose and a precursor to my work now as a Soul's Purpose Coach and Business Mentor who helps people discover and do what they came here for.

It worked!

I discovered I had a passionate interest! I discovered I had an insatiable curiosity with how people made changes in their lives! No one was more surprised than me!

I became one of those people I'd always admired – people who were passionate about their purpose in life and were constantly pursuing it. I became a mom. I became self-employed. I eventually met and married my husband. I created my own work, uncovered my own deep purpose and my unique and innate genius, and I started being the real me in all aspects of my life. For over twenty years, everything I've done for work and in my life has been to facilitate renewal and transformation by helping people see and claim their distinct beauty.

I answered my soul's calling.

I'm not telling you it was all easy or that I never had another day of discontent or questioning, but something HUGE shifted for me. I discovered my soul-self and let her into my life and let her guide me. I no longer felt that something was missing in my life.

> *Vocation does not come from a voice 'out there' calling me to be something I am not. It comes from a voice 'in here' calling me to be the person I was born to be, to fulfill the original selfhood given me at birth by God.*   *Parker Palmer*

People search their whole lives for their purpose, but they are looking in the wrong way or in the wrong places. You were never taught to listen to your soul in school. In fact, you were probably taught to follow the rules and NOT listen to your soul. To find what you were born to do, you'll need to "unlearn" many things rather than learn anything. Then you'll be able to see the threads woven into your life's tapestry that have always been there and point to your unique soul's purpose.

Over the last twenty years or so, I've worked with thousands of people and helped them hear and answer their own soul's calling.

My clients get aligned. They start being and doing what they came for – corporate consultants become healers, IT professionals become online program creators and teachers. My clients claim their own genius and use it to create the work that feeds their souls.

This is a magical time in history to create your own work and become a soul-inspired entrepreneur. Technology has made it possible for anyone who decides they want to, to create a micro-business and offer their original services via the Internet, the World Wide Web that connects us all. You can make a difference, make a living and share your unique gifts.

You'll learn to hear and answer the callings of your soul one tiny step at a time. Do these exercises in the order they are written, and you WILL figure out what you are here to do. I guarantee it!

I want you to find the peace, purpose and personal power you get when you live as your soul-self and not your ego-self.

Imagine if those of us that hear this call to soul, started answering it? Imagine the love and the dynamic power of creativity that would be unleashed in the world? Imagine the transformation and the renewal that would take place?

Can you imagine a world where everyone was using and sharing their unique genius? Can you imagine a world where people only did work they loved and no one was doing work only for power, prestige or money? Can you even conceive of that?

Imagine a world where people stopped pretending to be who they are not, and started expressing the beauty of who they actually are?

People would only do the work they loved. Teachers would teach, makers would make, scientists would explore, soul-guides would guide, legislators would legislate.

That's my dream: that we start a soul revolution; that we answer the call and bring more goodness, kindness and love into this world; that we do what we came here to do; that we stop hiding and stop thinking we can't; that we remember that we have divine instructions written in our own souls and all we have to do is learn how to hear and follow our soul's counsel; that we recognize that our tasks in the world all fit together in perfect harmony; that we remember that each of us is needed and essential just like the rest of the living beings in the world.

Imagine a world where you were doing what you were made for instead of doing what you could get paid for? Imagine being paid for what you can't NOT do?

It all starts with YOU.

I'm SO excited to share this with you. Have fun with this process!

Big love,

Bev.   *November 2016*

SOUL'S CALLING ROADMAP

THE SOUL'S CALLING ROADMAP   Created by Bev Barnes

www.bevbarnes.com

Take a look at the roadmap above. At the left there's a volcano. Imagine that you are living on that island, blissfully unaware that it is actually a volcano, and it erupts. You have to get off the island, get onto a boat and seek a new place to live. You must fundamentally shift your way of life.

This is the metaphor in the *Soul's Calling Roadmap*. It outlines the transition – the inner psychological process you make when you shift from living an ego-based (fake) life to living a soul-based (real) life. The transition from ego to soul is filled with endings, grief, unraveling, questioning and confusion. It involves the loss of the familiar. It can feel like walking blindfolded into the fog, not knowing what comes next. That's why I created the Soul's Calling Roadmap – so you'd feel a little less lost, so you'd be able to orient yourself, so that even when you are in the middle of unraveling your life, you'll know that you won't stay in this place forever.

The metaphor of the voyage off an island that is an erupting volcano, down to a beach, and then onto a boat whose destination is unknown appeared in my consciousness one day more than twenty-five years ago. I knew instinctively that this metaphor of an erupting volcano represented the transformation of consciousness the world would need to make. Now I know it is also a guide for your personal transformation to soul-based living.

Use the roadmap as your guide. Use it to orient yourself and give your mind something to hold onto when you are feeling lost.

Here's a more detailed description of the Soul's Calling Roadmap and the important lessons you need to learn as you move from the volcano to the boat.

1

1. S - Stop The Denial.

Dare to Decide to Leave the VOLCANO

Connect to Your Soul

The process of transformation begins when you recognize the volcano is erupting and you must leave the island. You have to dare to decide to leave the familiar island rather than denying what's really happening, that your home is being destroyed. The erupting volcano represents an ending, a major life event that changes you forever. Making the decision to leave the familiar (that isn't working) in search of the new (that might work better but you don't know for sure) IS the most important step in this process.

This is where you choose to embark on the process of change. You dare to decide to make a life change, to leave the old without knowing the new. You stop tolerating what you no longer want and stop denying that you are miserable in your current life.

You'll also need to learn to listen to your soul. You do this by starting a daily practice of listening to that deep, inner part of yourself. You'll begin to remember that you are a spiritual being having a human experience rather than pretending that you are a human being having a spiritual experience. That knowledge will help you to embark on the journey to soul.

2. O - Out Your Truth.

Sift Through the Sand on the BEACH to Uncover Your Truth

Answering your soul's calling doesn't happen overnight, and you'll spend much time out of your old life but not yet at your new life. The in-between time is visually represented on the roadmap as the beach. This is a time when you sift through the sand of your life and let go of what is *not* your truth. You *unpack* because you can't take anything on your trip that isn't yours. You'll leave behind outdated beliefs, rules, "shoulds" and anything that no longer serves you.

3. U - Unlock Your Unique Genius.

Find the Gems on the BEACH – Your Gifts, Your Passions and Your Soul's Purpose

On the beach you'll also find your gems – your most precious gifts and life themes which lead you straight to your soul's purpose. Your genius, which is the truth of who you are, will help you navigate the rest of your journey. Everyone has genius. On the beach you'll start to discover what you were made for. You'll once again need to dare to decide to move forward.

4. L - Lead With Love Not Fear.

CHOOSE A BOAT and Start the VOYAGE Using Your Soul as Your Compass and Guide

When you choose a boat, you shift from making your choices based on social rules or the ego, to making choices based on your soul's desires. You need to dare to decide again, and then take some small risk so you can begin the voyage. It's like jumping empty-handed into the void; you have absolutely no idea how the risk you are taking will work out – and you do it anyway.

Once you've set sail, the journey of living your life and navigating with your soul's desires is underway. While at first you think you are looking for a replacement island, it quickly becomes evident that you have begun a new adventure, living life as a boat dweller rather than a land dweller.

You discover you aren't looking for a new home but learning to live in a new way – one in which your ego is the helper rather than the leader. You are creating a life and work that is the best vehicle for your genius, and you are letting your soul guide you. Think of former U.S. President, Jimmy Carter in his nineties building houses at Habitat for Humanity. That is an example of someone who is letting his soul guide him.

The voyage *is* the destination.

The ego is now at the service of the soul rather than the other way around. On the voyage, you do the thing you were made for. You give your genius, find your courage and create. You practice and learn to be unattached to outcomes and to let your life lead you where it will.

This is a HUGE shift in the way we are taught to live. You can't do this alone. You'll need to be part of a like-minded community or tribe. The world as we know it, hasn't been set up for people following their soul's voice.

The voyage is an exercise in developing trust that your soul is always guiding you. Trusting that you are being guided by a benevolent force which wants only the best for you feels like surrendering control. You try things out, weather storms and stay on different islands, but you are constantly following your flow.

The metaphorical ocean itself is created from your desires and takes you in the direction your soul wants to go. As long as you let the current guide you and go with the flow, you'll be doing what you were made for. The ocean holds your destiny.

The journey flows with ease as long as you don't fight against the current. Use your genius, do the thing you were made for. Find or create your tribe and start *being* your soul-self in all aspects of your life.

3

The lighthouse symbolizes your soul's guidance. It lights the way and is always letting you know which way to go. In time, you will BE the lighthouse for others.

Where are you on the Soul's Calling Roadmap? The following exercise will help you to find your starting point.

EXERCISE 1: WHERE AM I ON THE SOUL'S CALLING ROADMAP?

PURPOSE:

- To get oriented and gain perspective on your situation;

- To use the roadmap metaphors to understand the process of finding and following your calling;

- To create safety and reduce anxiety about the process of transformation;

- To recognize you are in motion even when you think you aren't.

INSTRUCTIONS:

www.bevbarnes.com

1. Look at the **Soul's Calling Roadmap** above. You can download the Soul's Calling Roadmap here: bit.ly/SCRoadmap
   Answer the following questions:

   a. What is your volcano? Describe.

b. Where are you on the roadmap? Describe.

> [blank box]

* Come back to this exercise regularly to plot and understand your progress.

STOP THE DENIAL

Dare to Decide
Connect to Your Soul

DARE TO DECIDE

I have extraordinary coping abilities. They're what make me strong. However, because I can cope so well and for so long with pain, misery and suffering, it takes a long time for me to drop what I don't want and explore what I do want, and I don't ask for the help I really need. This is something I had to unlearn to find purpose and meaning in my life.

Are you one of those strong, silent types? Erupting on the inside while appearing as cool as a cucumber on the outside? Are you constantly repressing and suppressing your emotions because you've learned not to show yourself? That works in the world of ego but, in the world of soul, ignoring your emotions means you are blocking your inner guidance system.

You have to tell yourself the truth. You have to stop shoving down your misery. You don't have to vomit your emotions all over other people (in fact I really don't recommend that), but you do need to express them to yourself and maybe someone else who really sees you and understands you.

I thought that admitting I wasn't happy or that something wasn't working for me meant I had to have a plan to get out – of my job, of my relationship. I thought not expressing my misery was helping me to cope, and it was, but I was coping with the wrong life. Getting sick is the only result of coping for too long with something that your soul knows is wrong for you.

What I really needed was to stop denying my misery and pain, to stop trying so hard to cope with what I didn't want. That was the only way I could let it go. I had to stop pretending that all was well. This is absolutely the opposite of positive affirmations. I needed to allow myself to feel and to grieve and realize I wouldn't fall apart.

Nothing new can come into your life if you are expending all your energy trying to cope with something you don't want. To end stagnation and to have space for something new, you have to let something go; you have to surrender.

And there are no wrong decisions. Don't let your mind tell you that you'll be stuck forever if you make a wrong choice. There are no mistakes. Everything you do is *for* you.

I used to worry I might make the wrong decision, make a mistake or choose the wrong thing and be stuck there forever more. I was afraid to want something because suppose there was something better waiting around the corner that I hadn't seen yet?

Suppose Divine forces knew better than I did about what was right for me? Maybe I wouldn't let what was supposed to happen come about?

I wouldn't allow myself to want and I wouldn't allow myself to decide.

And then someone said to me something really, really simple.

> *You can always change your mind.*

What? You mean I can decide on something now and then, at some point, if it no longer feels right, I can make a new decision and follow that?

Of course.

You don't even have to know what you want yet. You just need to admit that what you are doing and how you are living, are no longer working. Period.

This quote by William H. Murray really helps me when I need to dare to decide:

Until one is committed, there is hesitancy, the chance to draw back, always ineffectiveness. Concerning all acts of initiative (and creation), there is one elementary truth, the ignorance of which kills countless ideas and splendid plans: that the moment one definitely commits oneself, then Providence moves too. All sorts of things occur to help one that would never otherwise have occurred. A whole stream of events issues from the decision, raising in one's favor all manner of unforeseen incidents and meetings and material assistance, which no man could have dreamt would have come his way.

The exercises that follow will help you to stop the denial and dare to decide to shift directions and let your soul guide you.

EXERCISE 2: DARE TO DECIDE

PURPOSE:

- To gain clarity on your current situation;

- To identify what is ending;

- To stop ignoring or repressing emotions and the information they hold;

- To start getting in touch with your soul's truths.

INSTRUCTIONS:

Answer some or all of these questions to gain more clarity on your current situation. Write your answers using your nondominant hand in the space provided.

1. Where is there a volcano erupting in my life?

2. Where have I abandoned my own needs and dreams?

3. What have I been coping with or tolerating?

[ ]

4. What's the payoff for not leaving this situation?

[ ]

5. What can I expect in my life if I never leave this situation?

[ ]

6. What does my soul know must be released?

[ ]

7. What am I grieving?

[ ]

8. What stories am I telling myself that are causing me to suffer?

[ ]

9. Why must I leave my comfort zone?

[ ]

EXERCISE 3: ONE TRANSITION IN DETAIL

DESCRIPTION:

Answering your soul's calling transforms the way you live your life. Transition is a 3-step inner emotional process that you go through when you deal with an external change event. It starts with an ending, followed by a period of being in limbo and then you move to the new beginning. You'll feel many emotions including grief, confusion, uncertainty, anger, and even excitement and hope. It can be overwhelming. You can learn how to best deal with transitions by looking at your past because the way you deal with any transition is the way you deal with every transition. That's what you'll do in this exercise.

PURPOSE:

- To help you identify your own way of handling life transitions;

- To give you safety and security and the ability to understand where you are in the transition process;

- To identify the strategies that help you manage transitions so you can incorporate these strategies into your life.

INSTRUCTIONS:

Think back on a major life change that is over. Choose a major change that you no longer have an emotional charge about, that you are no longer going through. It could be a move, a job change, the end of a relationship, etc.

Answer the questions about this change in the spaces provided below.

1. What emotions did you feel during this transition? List them.

2. What story did you tell yourself about this transition?

3. What did you do to cope with this transition? What worked and what didn't work?

4. How did you make sense of this process?

5. Summarize your process of dealing with life change. What you do, how you cope, the emotions you feel and how long it takes you to make the shift. This is the way that you make transitions. Use the strategies that help you as you are making this transition from ego to soul.

CONNECT TO YOUR SOUL

When in my 20s, I took a 5-day course on spiritual psychology. Our teacher asked us to listen to our inner voice. I wanted to ask her, "Which voice?" I knew I had a voice inside that was a constantly running inner commentary. This voice described everything I did and made assessments of what I said and how I behaved.

I'd been very shy as a teenager, and I didn't say much, so you'd assume I had lots of quiet and could hear this rumoured inner voice. Not true. Inside my head there was constant chatter. I got so tired of hearing the battling in my head, and I just wanted those voices to be quiet.

So when my teacher asked us to listen to our inner voice, I had no idea which voice she was talking about. It couldn't be the voice that was constantly telling me what to do. There had to be another voice I'd never heard.

There was.

There is a voice that comes from deep within you. It isn't chatter. It isn't bullying. It might not even be a voice. It's quiet, calm and sometimes directive. It's the voice that says *Don't get into that car* or *Why are you enrolled in biology when it bores you?* It's the way your body reacts when some thing, some place or some one feels like home, and you know without words where you belong.

That quiet voice – that isn't always a voice – is an energy that is always guiding you. It's the voice of your deep inner essence. It's the voice of your soul.

It doesn't compete with the running commentary in your head.

You need to be quiet to hear it, both on the inside and on the outside. The exercises that follow help you to develop a relationship with your soul.

EXERCISE 4: GROUNDING

Grounding is an essential practice for highly empathic people and highly sensitive people. It helps you connect to your body and focus yourself in an intentional and calming way. It helps you stay in your own energy and out of other people's energy.

PURPOSE:

- To help you connect to your body and focus yourself in an intentional and calming way;

- To get out of your mind and into your body;

- To create a habit of connecting to your soul.

INSTRUCTIONS:

Do this every day. Grounding is the fastest way to move out of your ego-self and into your soul-self. Become familiar with the sensation of being grounded.

1. Sit in a chair with your back straight and put your feet flat on the ground.

2. Close your eyes and take 12 deep belly breaths. Feel your belly rise on the inhale and fall on the exhale.

3. Imagine that beautiful roots are growing out of the bottoms of your feet and going down through the layers of soil and rock to attach you securely to the centre of the earth.

4. Feel the safety and connection of being in that place and being held by Mother Earth.

5. Stay with this for about 5 minutes.

6. When you are grounded, you'll hear less mind-chatter and feel like you're in your body rather than your mind. You'll be able to make decisions by checking into your body wisdom and escape the anxiety of a whirling, problem-solving, planning mind.

Download the audio for this exercise at:
http://bit.ly/groundbev/

EXERCISE 5: SOUL JOURNALING WITH THE SOUL'S CALLING CARDS

Soul journaling is a practice of tapping into your deepest inner truth in a playful and creative way. You can use soul journaling to ask a question. If you have my *Soul's Calling Cards**, you can use them in this exercise when you need guidance.

PURPOSE:

- To establish a trusting relationship with your soul;

- To develop a regular practice for getting your thoughts and your ego-self out of the way;

- To develop daily practices that feel like play and fun;

- To start to learn how your soul speaks to you;

- To get out of your ego-mind and into your soul-self;

- To access your soul's wisdom and counsel.

INSTRUCTIONS:

Get prepared with a journal and coloured markers, pencils or any other writing instrument that you like. Have your Soul's Calling Card Deck handy.

1. Ground yourself (see the previous exercise).

2. Pick a card with your nondominant hand and read it. If you don't have cards, write down a question you have for your Soul with your dominant hand.

3. Close your eyes, think about the question, and search in your heart for a response.

4. Write down your answer using your nondominant hand.

5. Draw a picture with your nondominant hand also, if you are so inclined.

6. If this feels like play, make this into a daily practice.

*Get the Soul's Calling Card Deck at: www. http://bit.ly/SCCardDeck

EXERCISE 6: THE TRUTH METER

DESCRIPTION:

This is arguably the most important exercise in this whole process: Learning the sensations in your body when it says Yes and when it says Yuck. If you followed these body signals and did only those things where your body said *Yes, Hell Yes*, you'd be hearing and answering your soul's calling. It really is *that* simple – but in our society, it's not that easy to do!

PURPOSE:

- To learn your body's signals for your soul's truths;

- To become familiar with your how your body guides you in the direction that your soul desires;

- To calibrate your soul's guidance system.

INSTRUCTIONS:

1. Think back and remember doing something you intensely disliked, in a place you disliked and/or around people that you disliked. Feel into your body and notice the physical sensations throughout your body as you imagine this.

2. Describe the physical sensations in your body. These are the words you associate with your strongest negative feelings.

3. List these words below on the left side of the chart under the negative numbers. This is your **"in prison"** feeling.

4. Now think back and remember doing something you loved or being with someone or in some place that you loved.

5. Describe the physical sensations your body has when you recall this experience. These are the words you associate with your strongest positive feelings.

6. List these words below on the right side of the chart under the positive numbers. This is your **"freedom"** feeling.

EXERCISE 6: THE TRUTH METER

Strongest Negative Feeling							Neutral							Strongest Positive Feeling						
-10	-9	-8	-7	-6	-5	-4	-3	-2	-1	0	+1	+2	+3	+4	+5	+6	+7	+8	+9	+10
YUCK!										YES!										

"In prison" body sensations	"Freedom" body sensations

* This exercise is based on Martha Beck's work in *Finding Your Own North Star: Claiming the Life You Were Meant to Live* and *Steering by Starlight: The Science and Magic of Finding Your Destiny.*

EXERCISE 7: BECOME THE SCIENTIST

PURPOSE:

- To practice using your Truth Meter:

- To start becoming aware of the messages you are getting from your body;

- To develop a relationship with your body and start following its counsel.

INSTRUCTIONS:

Complete this form three times per day. Practice noticing the sensations you feel in your body. How does your body speak to you? What messages does it send you on a regular basis?

COMPLETED EXAMPLE:

Time:
  10:00am

Body Sensations:
  Churning stomach and tightening in stomach

Rating on the Truth Meter:
  -4

Emotions:
Pick the emotion that is closest to one of these four emotions: Sad, Glad, Mad, Afraid
  Afraid, anxious

Circumstances:
  Meeting with my boss and colleagues about a program that we worked on that didn't work out well.

Message your body is giving you:
Don't worry about getting this right, just take a guess. Don't judge your answers.
  This situation isn't right for me. I really don't like working on this project or with these people.

Make several copies of the following exercise and complete it three times per day.

EXERCISE 7: BECOME THE SCIENTIST

* Make several copies of this form

INSTRUCTIONS:

Complete this form three times per day. Practice noticing the sensations you feel in your body. How does your body speak to you? What messages does it send you on a regular basis?

Time:

Body Sensations:

Rating on the Truth Meter:

Emotions:
Pick the emotion that is closest to one of these four emotions: Sad, Glad, Mad, Afraid

Circumstances:
Describe the situation

Message your body is giving you:
Don't worry about getting this right, just take a guess. Don't judge your answers.

OUT YOUR TRUTH

Commit to Congruence
Make Up Your Own Life Rules

COMMIT TO CONGRUENCE

When I was in my corporate job, I was wearing a mask every day and not being the real me. I just didn't fit. I wondered what was wrong with me. I felt like an alien who spoke a different language and came from a different land than most of my co-workers. As soon as I stepped into the workplace, I became the person who I was hired to be and the real me, my essence, disappeared.

In our workplace, corporate culture dictated that if you were at a managerial level, when you wrote memos, you didn't sign them. Your boss, the director, did. I must have written hundreds of memos that were all signed by my boss, where my name was erased along with any evidence of me. Those ghost memos, signed by my boss though written by me, were a perfect representation of me in that workplace. I didn't exist. My essence was invisible.

I looked around, and other people seemed fine. They didn't complain or resent their "disappearance" into the corporate ether. I wondered what was wrong with me that this all felt "wrong" to me. I didn't know what to do about it. I was a dormant volcano – erupting on the inside but not letting anyone know.

My last straw was at an out-of-town corporate meeting. I was in a hotel ballroom – one of those no-windowed, Persian-carpeted, fluorescent-lit, nameless hotel ballrooms. This time I heard it. My soul was screaming, wanting out. I was surrounded by men and women in suits arguing about something that I didn't care about, that had nothing to do with anything.

I decided I couldn't waste my time there any longer. In a moment of rebellion, I left. Like Paul Simon sang: I snuck out the back, Jack. I didn't have a plan, Stan. I just wanted to be free.

I didn't go back to that meeting.

I hopped on a street-car, stopped for a latte and made my way through the shops, ending up at a small self-help bookstore.

Oh, sweet freedom. I could finally breathe.

A quiet bookstore, indie music, self-help books.

The mask was off. I was finally being myself.

And that's when I knew I had to start being me in all aspects of my life. I had no idea where it would lead, but I had to do this. There was no other way.

That's what your soul wants for you: *Congruence* – being the same person on the outside as you are on the inside. The exercises that follow will help you start becoming congruent.

EXERCISE 8: MISERY BOARD

DESCRIPTION:

Most people have heard of vision boards, but have you ever done a misery board? A misery board is a great way to get to clear psychic space. You stop pretending you are happy or satisfied with your current circumstances and you allow yourself to express that in a collage. Your misery board is a collage that represents the things in your current life that deplete your spirit.

Once that collage is done, it's easy to see that what you really desire is the opposite of your misery board. Afterward, you can do the Felt Sense Collage exercise that follows and get even clearer on what you desire.

PURPOSE:

- To help you express and release your misery;

- To use the contrast of what you *don't* want to help you discover what you *do* want;

INSTRUCTIONS:

1. **Prepare:**

   Get a piece of poster board and a selection of magazines, scissors and glue sticks, and plan for at least one hour of undisturbed time. I don't recommend doing your collage online. That is a whole different process focused on selecting without the ripping, tearing, gluing and sticking you can do with real magazines. It's less satisfying when you don't "make" with your hands so, whenever possible, do your collage using magazines, photos and other concrete materials you can touch.

2. **Ground:**

   Take 10 deep belly breaths. As you breathe in, notice your belly rise and your belly fall as you breathe out (not the other way around).

3. **Find Your Question:**

Ask yourself a question. Here are a few examples. Choose one or create your own.

- What have I been coping with for far too long?
- Where has the elastic of my soul lost her ability to stretch?
- What do I no longer want in my life?
- What is making me miserable now?

4. **Rip or cut out pictures and words that respond to your question:**

Allow yourself to express your emotions. You may find that you are feeling angry or sad or self-righteous. Every emotion is allowed. Don't stifle yourself. You are allowing yourself to express discontent.

5. **Arrange and then glue your images and words to your board:**

Don't analyze or think about trying to make your collage say something – let this remain a mystery. If there are images that no longer fit, don't use them.

6. **Look at your collage and respond to these questions:**

a. **What do I no longer want in my life?**
Example: When I did this exercise, my collage was black and white. There was lots of space between the pictures. It was clear I no longer wanted a life that was colourless and connectionless.

b. **What do I need to create in my life?**
Example: I needed to create more colour, travel, people and places, and I needed more connection with people.

EXERCISE 9: FELT SENSE COLLAGE

EXPLANATION:

Now that you've done a misery board, the Felt Sense Collage will be much easier! A felt sense collage is one based on the feelings you want to have rather than the things you want to achieve. When you focus on how you want to feel rather than what you want to have, you widen the opportunities that come your way and sometimes achieve even more than you ever hoped for!

This is the collage I made when I imagined being a Life Coach and being the same person on the inside as I was on the outside. This is one way to set your intention without doing a paper-and-pencil thinking exercise.

PURPOSE:

- To help you set a clear intention;

- To help you make conscious choices;

- To discover that underneath your desires lays how you want to *feel*, which is your true objective;

- To tap into your nonverbal right brain and use its wisdom;

- To anchor the way you want to feel by creating a visual representation of it.

INSTRUCTIONS:

1. **Prepare:**

   Get a piece of poster board and a selection of magazines, scissors and glue sticks, and plan for at least one hour of undisturbed time. I don't recommend doing your collage online. That is a whole different process focused on selecting without the ripping, tearing, gluing and sticking you can do with real magazines. It's less satisfying when you don't "make" with your hands so, whenever possible, do your collage using magazines, photos and other concrete materials you can touch.

2. **Ground:**

   Take 10 deep belly breaths. As you breathe in, notice your belly rise and your belly fall as you breathe out (not the other way around).

3. **Find Your Question:**

   What question do you want the answer to? My question on the collage above was *What do I want in my coaching biz?* Your question could be *Who am I becoming?* or *How do I want to feel?* or *What inspires me?* or anything else that shows up for you.

4. **Rip or cut out pictures and words that respond to your question:**

   Only pull out images and words that open your heart and feel like LOVE.

5. **Arrange and then glue your images and words to your board:**

Stay in your heart as you arrange your pictures and words. Don't analyze or think about trying to make your collage say something – let this remain a mystery. If there are images that no longer fit, don't use them.

6. **Look at your collage and respond to these questions:**

   a. **How does this collage make me feel? Pick 3 descriptors.**
   My collage makes me feel joyful, inspired and incredibly grateful. Write your answers below.

   b. **Ask yourself *Who am I becoming?* as you look at your collage.**
   This is a powerful question. The answers will inspire you. Write your answers below.

EXERCISE 10: SET YOUR INTENTION

EXPLANATION:

A statement of intention is not a goal; it is an aim that guides action. It's gentle and keeps you focused in the present moment. It is concerned with *being* rather than *doing* and does not foster lavish expectations or rigid agendas. It is *process* rather than *outcome*-focused.

My intention when I began the journey to hear and answer my soul's calling was: *I intend to be congruent – the same person on the outside as I am on the inside.* Setting this intention and using the Truth Meter, were the two things that were most useful to me in figuring out why I was here.

As Deepak Chopra explains, everything that happens in the universe begins with intention. Thousands of years ago, the sages of India observed that our destiny is ultimately shaped by our deepest intentions and desires.

PURPOSE:

-   To help you create a powerful intention based on a current situation;

-   To shift your energy by removing the blocks to attracting what you want;

-   To integrate information that comes from your emotions and felt senses into your desires;

-   To tap into your body's wisdom!

INSTRUCTIONS:

1. Identify an area of deep discontent or dissatisfaction.
    For example: I am so tired of feeling like a prisoner in my relationship.

2. Ask yourself *What no longer serves me?* Dig deep and find your soul's truth. Write that down or draw an image with your nondominant hand below.
For example: telling myself that I am stuck and have no choice.

3. **Find your truth. Set an intention that is stated in positive terms.**
For example: I intend to find my freedom and move towards it.

4. **Check in with your body to see if you have discovered the intention that feels powerful.** If it does you'll feel energized and a sense of your heart opening. If it doesn't, you'll feel depleted and have a heavy heart. Find a better intention, if needed, and write that down below.

MAKE UP YOUR OWN LIFE RULES

We all have expectations placed on us from the moment we are born. I was the second child of two, and I was expected to be my sister's playmate. At two years old I knew I was going to University. This was my parent's dream. Growing up in Canada at a time when there were few people of colour, I was expected not to make waves, not to call attention to myself, to fit into the dominant culture.

I learned what everyone's expectations of me were – my friends, my family, my teachers. When I saw my sister getting hurt or rejected, I learned what not to do – put myself out there. Being empathic was an advantage and helped me learn what others expected of me really quickly, but I was completely out of touch with what I wanted.

When you spend your life following other peoples' rules and fitting in, you stop hearing the whispers of your own soul, desire, curiosity, interest, passion. Without those whispers, you don't know what you want, and life feels meaningless.

My parents were proud to see me as the scientist in the family. I was good at math and science, so I was expected to go into the sciences like all good students of my era. But I hated chemistry labs. I hated every single part of a chemistry lab – the calculations, the experiments. So what did I do? I applied and got accepted to McGill University in biology – a subject I disliked only slightly less than chemistry. I did end up switching to psychology before I began my university studies, but most 17-year-olds make decisions about what to do with their lives based on the opinions of those who have the most influence over them. That kind of decision-making will lead you far off your own path because no one else knows what lights you up.

The rules we follow are well-intentioned, for the most part. The people we love want the best for us. I'm thrilled my parents wanted me to have an education and be financially independent. But do I really have to always pretend that all is well, even when it isn't?

The first step to making up your own life rules is to become aware of the rules you are following subconsciously, and then check in with your body. Do these life rules energize you or deplete you?

Do the thoughts you are thinking support you and move you in the direction of your soul or do they bring you down and move you towards your socialized, ego-driven self?

Noticing your mind-chatter, thoughts, beliefs and rules, and then questioning them and evaluating whether they hurt or hinder you, is what you'll do in these exercises.

When you unclutter your mind, there is a much clearer channel to your soul, and you can hear her whispers trying to guide you.

EXERCISE 11: WHOSE DREAM IS THIS?

PURPOSE:

- To become aware of who has influenced your choices and how;

- To consciously choose the influences you want to maintain and those you want to drop.

INSTRUCTIONS:

1. Jot down the names of everyone in your family and extended family plus anyone who was important to you when you were growing up, such as teachers, coaches, neighbors, cousins, older friends, etc.

2. Draw a stick figure of each person you listed and write their name above their stick figure.

3. Underneath each stick figure, write ONE thing they wanted from you. Don't think too much and don't even be concerned if you are not absolutely sure this is what they wanted from you. What is most important is *your perceptions,* not whether you were right or wrong.

In one long sentence, summarize each item on this list. Start your sentence with: *I am supposed to be...*

4. Now, test each message against your own soul's truth using your Truth Meter. List each of your "shoulds" in the left-hand column. Check in with your body and your Truth Meter. Ask yourself *Is this message **my** soul's truth?* If not, what is your soul's truth around that issue? Write that down in the right-hand column.

"Shoulds" that are NOT your soul's truth:	Beliefs that ARE your soul's truth:

* This exercise is inspired by Barbara Sher's *I Could Do Anything If I Only Knew What It Was: How to Discover What You Really Want and How to Get It.*

EXERCISE 12: UNCLUTTER YOUR MIND

It's important that you get your mind out of its own way so you can hear your soul's calling. You'll learn how to coach yourself by using this process. Coaching yourself means becoming aware of when you are feeling discomfort and gently asking yourself questions so you can discover your truth and then act on that.

PURPOSE:

- To develop a regular practice for getting your thoughts and your ego-self out of the way so you can hear and answer your soul's calling;

- To help you gain awareness of the stories you tell yourself that aren't true;

- To help you notice that behind painful emotions lays a story that is not your soul's truth;

- To discover your soul's truth – big "L" love – rather than your ego's truth.

- To get out of your ego-mind and into your soul-self;

- To access your soul's wisdom and counsel.

INSTRUCTIONS:

1. **Notice when you are feeling misery, discomfort or emotional pain.**

2. **Ask yourself _Why am I feeling misery, discomfort or emotional pain?_**
Do a mind dump and write down all your answers. Do not censor filter yourself, just get it all out and write it down.

Example:
I am feeling very stressed about not quitting my job which I hate. I think I should quit because I know I'm not really doing what lights me up, but I'm afraid I'll go broke or not find another job and I'm nervous about starting a business because who would buy my services. This job just gets worse and worse every day. Am I just supposed to cope with this? Is this what people do all their lives? I'll never get out of this situation, I'll be stuck here forever because I don't know what else I could do and I'm too afraid to quit.

3. **Give your untrue story a name.**

Example:
This is my "NOTHING WILL EVER CHANGE" story.

4. **Ask yourself these questions:**

   a. When I believe my miserable story, how do I feel?
   Describe your body sensations below.

b. When I believe my miserable story, what do I do?

c. When I believe my miserable story, how do I treat myself?

d. When I believe my miserable story, how do I treat others?

e. When I believe my miserable story, what am I forgetting or ignoring?

f. Finally, ask yourself *Does believing my miserable story move me closer to big "L" LOVE or further away from that love? Is this story my soul's truth?*

```



```

5. **Remember a time when you felt big "L" love, a time when you were in your element doing something that you love, in a place you love, with a child you love or with a pet you love.**

Sink deeply into those feelings and spend a couple of minutes checking into your body and noticing where those feelings reside. Describe the experience and your body sensations below.

Example:
Ease and flow, like I'm floating and smiling and content. My heart feels open.

```



```

6. **Now, ask yourself *What's my soul's truth? What's a kinder, gentler, truer story that leads me closer to my soul's truth?* Write that down here.**

Example:
I'm so excited about learning more about what I love. I've discovered that I have this natural talent to help people shift the way they see difficult situations (how ironic). Even though I don't like this job, I'm not stuck here. I'm working towards getting clear on what I'm talented at, so I can start to use my talents more. I'm not stuck, I'm discovering my gifts and finding ways to use them.

```



```

7. Identify one tiny step you can take, one tiny act of courage you can take now, that will lead you closer to your heart's desires and feels like freedom. Write that down below – and then do it!

Example:
I can go and talk to the person that does training in our company and find out more about what she does. It is something that interests me.

Your soul's truth ALWAYS feels like freedom!

* This exercise is inspired by Byron Katie's *Loving What Is: Four Questions That Can Change Your Life.*

UNLOCK YOUR OWN UNIQUE GENIUS

Claim Your Innate Gifts and Your Soul's Purpose

CLAIM YOUR INNATE GIFTS AND YOUR SOUL'S PURPOSE

My corporate job was a real life-lesson lab. My soul put together so many miserable experiences that I needed to learn from – all in one place. One of those lessons was about my own value and my own genius.

I had a small staff of recent university grads. This was their first job and, while I was only a little older than them, I was a corporate veteran. I decided I'd help them develop and grow, and shift their self-identity from student to professional. I also wanted to discover what they did best so they could start doing more of that and less of what they didn't like or weren't strong at. I created all kinds of innovative exercises and practices to do with them, taking insight from my library of self-help books. It was the most fun thing I did on my job.

One day it was time for my yearly performance appraisal. I sat down with my boss, expecting she would give me feedback about the great work my team was doing. I did get great feedback, but she didn't mention my work with the recent grads, so I asked her. What she said stupefied me and totally changed my life.

She said, "You are doing great work with them, but that's not in your job description. It isn't what you are paid to do." Now, I could have made all kinds of arguments about how developing people changes everything we do, but I think I was just shocked. I said nothing.

And I had a clear soul message:

> *You are not valued for what you do best.*
> *Decide to find work where you are valued for your own genius.*

And that's what I decided to do.

Before you figure out whether you can use and share and give your genius, you've got to become aware of what it is.

The exercises that follow will help you do that.

EXERCISE 13: TOP TEN PRIDE STORIES

PURPOSE:

- To connect with the positive feelings you have when you are using your innate gifts;

- To clarify what your gifts are;

- To notice how you feel physically when you are using your gifts;

- To identify your values and your passions;

- To start identifying your personal criteria for success and what you really want;

- To help you distinguish the feelings of essence-based pride versus ego-based pride.

DESCRIPTION:

This exercise asks you to look at the things in your life that you are most proud of – not in an ego sense but in your heart. This could be something you did, a way you behaved or a time you felt enveloped with love. We often think of the word "pride" as being associated with public acclaim and related to egocentricity. This isn't necessary for this exercise.

INSTRUCTIONS:

In a heart-expanding way, look at the things you have felt really proud of. You may or may not have received recognition for what you did. What's most important is the way your heart expands when you remember the story.

STEPS:

1. Go through your life in 7-year segments (0-7, 7-14, etc.) and note down what you were proud of during that time segment. It doesn't have to be anything that someone else noticed. For example, I was proud that I stopped sucking my fingers at twelve years old after believing I couldn't do it. List as many as you can.

2. Now go through your list and pick out your top 10 pride stories. Check in with your body. Choose pride stories that make your heart open, that make you feel light and free when you think about them, not those that make you feel tight and constricted.

   Your pride stories can be small or big, affect only you or other people, too. You can select events that happened a long time ago or very recently. Select them based on the joy and satisfaction you felt and the pride you feel in recalling them.

3. Give each story a provocative title. Write the titles in the space below:

MY TOP TEN PRIDE STORIES:

1. _____

2. _____

3. _____

4. _____

5. _____

6. _____

7. _____

8. _____

9. _____

10. _____

EXERCISE 14: DIVE DEEPER!

PURPOSE:

- To define your gifts more clearly using words;

- To identify what you really value most or what is most important in your pride stories;

- To distinguish between your skills, your unique talents and gifts, and your values;

- To help you see you are gifted at what you love!

- To help identify what is most meaningful to you.

INSTRUCTIONS:

Complete the chart below for each of your top ten pride stories. Write a brief description of each pride story and answer the questions, use more paper if you need to.) When you choose your pride stories, choose those that expand and open your heart. Pick your stories using your soul-self, not your social-self.

Answer these questions about each pride story:

- Why were you proud? (These are your values)

- What talents or gifts or qualities did it take to accomplish this? (These are parts of your genius)

- What did you particularly enjoy doing? (This is a key part of your genius)

Photocopy the following page 10 times and complete it for each story.

PRIDE STORIES: DIVE DEEPER!

Story #_____	
Provocative Title	
Description	
Why I'm Proud *Your Values*	
Talents or Gifts I Used *Parts of Your Genius*	
What I Loved Doing *Your Passions*	

EXERCISE 15: SUMMARY OF STORIES

PURPOSE:

- To summarize what you found about your values, gifts and passions in the pride stories;

- To start seeing the thread of your unique genius that weaves through your life.

INSTRUCTIONS:

1. Review your answers in the Pride Story and Dive Deeper exercises then complete the spaces below.

   My Values (why I'm proud):

   My Genius (talents or gifts I used):

   My Passions (what I loved doing):

EXERCISE 16: THE PASSION QUESTIONS

PURPOSE:

- To name your passions;

- To find your heart's true desires;

- To get even clearer on what you value and what is meaningful to you!

INSTRUCTIONS:

1. **Answer the following questions:**

   a. What are you doing when you get so absorbed that you lose all track of time?
   b. What do you absolutely love learning about?
   c. What conversations do you overhear and ache to join in?
   d. If you could switch lives with someone, who would you pick? Why?
   e. What are people always asking you to help them with? What do you naturally do well?
   f. Who do you admire or envy most? Why?
      Envy is often a signal that you aren't doing something you want to.
   g. Have you ever been engaged in an activity and felt like it was "coming through you"? That you were exerting no effort and still getting all the results you desired? What were you doing?
      This is the clearest signal that you are using your genius.
   h. Describe a time when you were at your best, doing what you love, in a place you love, with the people you love.
   i. If you could change anything in the world, what would that be? Why?
   j. What are you doing when you're procrastinating?

2. **Summarize your findings in one paragraph:**

EXERCISE 17: LET YOUR LIFE SPEAK, PART 1

PURPOSE:

- To become aware of the specific lessons life has been teaching you;

- To find the theme or core message of your life;

- To uncover your soul's purpose through these life lessons and your core theme.

INSTRUCTIONS:

1. Consider the life experiences and changes that occurred in each of your seven-year cycles. Jot down a few notes beside the appropriate circle.

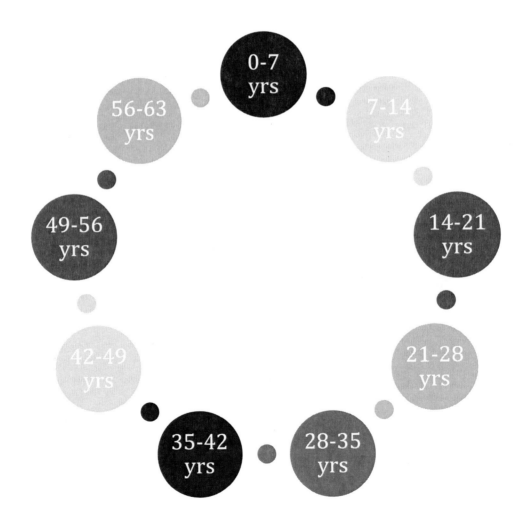

EXERCISE 18: LET YOUR LIFE SPEAK, PART 2

INSTRUCTIONS:

1. Answer these questions for each 7-year period of your life. If you need more seven-year periods than provided, just use a notebook. This exercise will take some quiet reflection, so choose a time when you are relaxed and can complete this without interruption.

    a. Briefly describe the circumstances of your life for this 7-year period.

    b. What was most difficult in this 7-year period?

    c. What was the theme of this 7-year period?

    d. Looking back, what lesson do you think that life, or your soul, wanted you to learn? *You are given the lessons that are the opposite of what you need to learn. For example, if your theme was being constantly afraid, your soul is teaching you how to connect to your courage. If you were always alone, your soul is teaching you that you are never alone. What lesson was your soul teaching you?*

Here is an example of my completed 7- to 14-year-old age period:

> 1. Circumstances: We moved to Canada. I had a British accent and was a tiny black girl in a white society.
>
> 2. Most difficult life experiences: I was worried about not fitting in, not knowing the rules, being "different". I wanted desperately to fit in and not be noticed and be accepted and liked.
>
> 3. Theme - Adapt! Fit in!
>
> 4. My soul wanted me to learn to stop hiding and be me — that I mattered and I needed to stand out and shine.

Now complete yours on the following page! Use additional paper if necessary.

0-7 yrs

7-14 yrs

14-21 yrs

21-28 yrs

28-35 yrs

35-42 yrs

42-49 yrs

49-56 yrs

56-63 yrs

EXERCISE 19: SOUL'S PURPOSE - CORE MESSAGE

PURPOSE:

- To become aware of the specific lessons that life has been teaching you;

- To find the theme or core message of your life;

- To uncover your soul's purpose through these life lessons and your core theme.

INSTRUCTIONS:

1. What big themes/issues have repeated themselves over and over again in your life?

2. What are the three most important lessons you have learned in your life?

3. What is the biggest problem you have overcome in your life?

4. What is the one core message or theme that emerges from your life lessons and these questions? This is likely your soul's purpose! Write that down below.

EXERCISE 20: SOUL'S CALLING BLUEPRINT

PURPOSE:

- To have a one-page guide that will help you choose a boat and navigate your soul's calling journey;

- To create a document that outlines your own definition of success.

INSTRUCTIONS:

1. Complete the following questions. Use what you have discovered in the exercises you have already completed.

2. Add pictures, art and colours to make this blueprint your own. Keep it in a space that you go to every day.

My criteria for success include:

a. Using my top three talents or gifts of:
   Use your pride stories to complete this.

   _____

   _____

   _____

b. Remaining aligned with the top three values of this stage in my life:
   Use the values you identified in your pride stories to complete this.

   _____

   _____

   _____

c. Expressing my passions and interests in:
Use the responses you found in the Passion questions to complete this.

```




```

d. Sharing my **core message** that:
Use the core message that you identified here.

```




```

My soul is calling me to:

```




```

My personal style is:
Use 3 adjectives that describe your style in the world. For example: fun, playful and elegant.

```




```

A quotation that inspires me is:

```
┌─────────────────────────────────────────────────┐
│                                                 │
│                                                 │
│                                                 │
│                                                 │
│                                                 │
│                                                 │
└─────────────────────────────────────────────────┘
```

Now pull it all together in a paragraph as follows:

My criteria for success includes using my talents and gifts of _____,
_____ and _____. I need to remain aligned with my top 3 values
of _____, _____, and _____, and I am passionate about
_____, _____, and _____. I intend to share my core message
of _____, which is also my soul's purpose in this life.

Right now, my soul is calling me to _____ and to do this is a way that expresses
my _____ and _____ style.

" _____ "

Completed Soul's Calling Blueprint Example:

My criteria for success includes using my gift of essence seeing; holding safe-space and facilitating/ coaching transformation and change. I need to remain aligned with my top 3 values, living in my truth, constantly growing and developing, and the freedom to create the life I want. I am passionate about purpose, transformation and that humanity needs to evolve. I intend to share my core message: It's time to stop hiding; the world needs your genius, now — which is also my soul's purpose in this life.

Right now my soul is calling me to make this work more accessible to more people and to do this in a fun, playful and elegant way.

"There is a vitality, a life force, an energy, a quickening that is translated through you into action, and because there is only one of you in all time, this expression is unique. And if you block it, it will never exist through any other medium and will be lost." Martha Graham

Write your own Soul's Calling Blueprint on the following page.

MY SOUL'S CALLING BLUEPRINT

LEAD WITH LOVE NOT FEAR

**Follow Your Joy
Do It Afraid!**

FOLLOW YOUR JOY

Once I made a commitment to be congruent, to dare to decide to discover what I loved to do, to make my own life rules and unlock my own genius, I had found a thread to follow. I finally knew what I liked – personal and professional development.

I was totally curious about how people actually made changes in their lives. One day, when I took a look at my bookshelf, I finally saw the obvious – I had shelves of life purpose and self-help books. Clearly, purpose and life transformation were my passionate interests.

Now I needed to do something. I wanted to immerse myself in the world of personal development. I was on fire by this time, setting up interviews to talk to people about their work, discovering fields like outplacement (that I'd never heard of) which seemed to be something made for me. I was investigating the profession of coaching, which was in its infancy then. I was following anything and everything that I was curious about without attachment to the outcome, seeing which path was right for me, even as I stayed in my job. I didn't quit my job because I still didn't know what I wanted to do but I was definitely making progress.

It finally hit me that I needed to get more training in counseling or applied psychology. I knew my soul's work involved helping people in this way. I had always done this, for all my life, and it was one of my true and unique gifts but, without any training, I couldn't present myself to the world as a helper/guide (so I thought).

I decided to interview professors because I've always loved school. I wanted to know whether I needed more training to coach people about their purpose and their mission. I knew that while discussing purpose, you often get into very deeply hidden places, like past trauma and unresolved grief, and I wanted to make sure I would do no harm.

I arranged meetings with a psychology professor and a professor of education who taught counseling psychology. The meeting with the psychology professor felt like my meetings at work – boring. When I walked into the education professor's office, it felt like one of those magical moments when I could feel the air on my skin, where we were both totally present, and I got a little dizzy. It felt like an energy vortex rush. We'd talked for about five minutes and then he got up and said, "Come with me." I followed him wordlessly. He took me to the registration desk and said to the receptionist, "Sign her up for my class." He didn't ask me. I had no idea what his class was. I looked at him quizzically. "You need to be in my class. Sign up. It's on Mondays," he said.

And I did.

It was a graduate course called Vocational Choice and Development. It answered every question I'd asked Dr. Phil Patsula. When I walked into that class, I felt like I was home. I still had my job. I was taking a daytime class on Mondays with the complete approval of my boss.

I knew my voyage had begun.

The language of the soul is joy. The soul speaks to you with fun, play, joy, expansion, smiles and sunlight. It feels like openness, expansion, flying and being lit up.

You can't just think about your soul or feel it in meditation. You have to *do* something.

Answering your soul's calling means listening to your soul's whispers and doing something – renting a studio, creating a card deck, taking a class you're interested in, trying your hand at painting or yoga or something you've never done but it's been calling you.

Once you take a small action that your soul is directing you to take, it will lead to something else you'll only see after you take that small action. It's like moving through the fog and the next step becomes clear only when you are right in front of it – and you can't see beyond that.

The soul does not make her plans visible to you. You've got to start moving.

When you start moving you'll see the next steps you need to take, but not before. As you keep taking steps, you'll stumble upon your purpose, and you'll create that service that is aligned with your soul.

You must take action; you can't just think about it. Nothing is a mistake. If something doesn't work, that just gives you more information about what tweaks to make so that it works better. It is a process of shifting, changing and refining while you are moving forward.

Do something that your soul is whispering for you to do! The following exercises will help you to choose your actions.

EXERCISE 21: CREATE A TINY PASSION PROJECT

PURPOSE:

- To start taking action and answer your soul's calling;

- To outwit your fear by taking a tiny step;

- To create a passion project that comes from your soul and not from your ego.

INSTRUCTIONS:

It's time to start working on something you love. It could be anything. The goal is to create something that allows you to use your genius in a really tiny, easy, non-threatening way.

Have an idea?

Great! Write it down here:

No ideas or too many ideas? Do this:

1. Go for a walk.

2. Formulate the question you want the answer to before your walk. Here are a few examples: *What tiny passion project needs to be created right now? What tiny project would be fun to do?* Say it out loud.

3. Do not focus on the question as you walk, just intend to return with an answer. If you find yourself obsessively scouring for a response, just push those thoughts aside and focus on the present moment – your breathing, your steps, what you see, etc.

4. Walk for at least one half hour. Don't use a music device.

5. Upon your return, list the ideas you have for a passion project. No ideas? Be patient. Repeat this exercise. An idea will appear.

DO IT AFRAID!

I used to think I was more afraid than anyone. I used to think I had to deal with my fear, get rid of it before I moved forward in my life or did anything about making changes in my life.

You feel afraid and do it anyway.

That's how you develop your courage muscle. Being downsized pushed me to decide. Yes, I'd been on my soul's path, but I was holding on to my job and, once again, I didn't decide to end it, my soul did. I was downsized. Actually, I wasn't just downsized; the volcano of my life erupted, and I had no job, no relationship and a baby on the way.

Then I realized something.

Fear is only a problem when you are anticipating some off-in-the-future event. When you are actually in the situation you fear, you get focused, and you get going. I asked myself right away: *Do I want to search for another job that is similar to my old job? Because I could, it'd be easy.*

Or did I want to create my own career the way I really wanted it to be, my own soul-based business?

I got super-clear on how I wanted to live, that I wanted to be a mom – even alone – and I ended up buying a house, starting a business and becoming a mom all at the same time.

Someone said to me at the time, "Now you are really not afraid!" That was SO not the truth. I was afraid, and I did it anyway.

That's how I discovered I was brave – by being afraid and doing it anyway.

I don't doubt my courage anymore. I still get afraid; it's part of being human.

Do it afraid. There isn't any choice.

The following exercises help you become more conscious of your own way of dealing with fear so that you don't let fear stop you from answering your soul's calling.

EXERCISE 22: YOUR FEAR STYLE

PURPOSE:

- To recognize that you have a preferred style when dealing with fear;

- To help you recognize your fear behaviors;

- To give you effective fear-busting strategies.

INSTRUCTIONS:

Read the descriptions below about two different styles of responding to fear. Identify which style resembles you the most and answer the questions below.

Freezer Description:

Freezers try to hide from fear by standing still. Freezers are like a deer in headlights. They procrastinate, self-analyze and don't act on their great ideas. They fall into self-doubt and wait to act until they feel better. Often by the time they take action, their passion has waned. They heap on self-criticism, self-flagellation and despair, and they compare themselves unfavorably with others who get more done. They fall into resistance and shift the focus from their desires by becoming obsessed with things like how to lose weight, organizing the kitchen and binge-watching *on Netflix*.

They have a tendency towards "rust out", not using or developing their gifts.

Tornado Description:

Tornados try to outrun their fear. They avoid feeling fear by constantly being in motion, by doing. They feed on the adrenaline. They are like swashbuckling pirates, ignoring their physical needs, taking on every challenge, doing and accomplishing. They get much praise for all they accomplish but they lose pleasure in their accomplishments and often become experts in things they aren't interested in. They feel overwhelmed and overworked and often complain that they don't have enough time.

They have a tendency towards "burnout", which can be the only time they permit themselves to stop.

1. Which is your fear style? Neither is better than the other.

```



```

2. Describe a time when you displayed this fear style. Describe the circumstances, your feelings, your thoughts and your behavior.

```



```

Freezer Fear-busting Strategy (DECIDE – DO – FEEL):

Freezers get derailed by overthinking and not taking action. They need to DECIDE what they want – by making sure their intention is aligned with their soul's truth and then DO the thing. Their final step is to FEEL – checking in with the body's Truth Meter to determine if they need to tweak their action in some way. Freezers need to remember to DO.

Tornado Fear-busting Strategy (DECIDE – FEEL – DO):

Tornados get derailed by doing too much and not doing what their soul desires. They need to DECIDE what they want – by making sure their intention is aligned with their soul's truth. Then they need to FEEL, by checking in with the body's Truth Meter to determine if the action lights them up or needs tweaking. Then, they can DO the thing. Tornados need to remember to FEEL, by checking into their body's Truth Meter.

EXERCISE 23: EMBRACE AND LEARN FROM YOUR FEAR

PURPOSE:

- To help you create a new story about fear;

- To help you decide to shift your response to fear;

- To become aware of the story you have been telling yourself about answering your soul's calling;

- To identify beliefs you may be unaware of;

- To determine whether these beliefs support or block you from creating your life's work;

- To help you to start consciously choosing your beliefs;

- To start telling your truth.

INSTRUCTIONS:

Use this worksheet when you feel fear about something you need to do to answer your soul's calling. **You can download a recording of this exercise, at** http://bit.ly/fearbev. Do the following:

1. **Stop the denial.** What is the situation you are pretending you're okay with or trying to deny is painful or fear-invoking? Note it down below:

2. **Observe and feel the fear.** First observe the fear in your body from the outside. Then sink into your body and feel those body sensations, even if you don't like them, for 90 seconds. Describe where you feel these sensations and what you feel. Notice how the sensations shift throughout the 90 seconds.

3. **Ask your fear what it needs.** You might get a clear response – like you need to prepare some material right away – or you might not get anything. That's fine. If you get instructions, note them down below and decide whether or not you will follow them.

4. **Out your ego.** Notice any thoughts or stories that come up as you are feeling your fear. Examples are *I'll never be able to do this,* or *I'm not good enough,* etc. Write them down below.

5. **Uncover your soul's truth.** Do this by shaking off the fear and imagining a past situation where you felt pure love. An easy way to do this is to remember a time when you were in your element and sharing your unique genius. Now go back to the original fear situation and, from this perspective of love, ask yourself *What is my deepest truth about this situation?* Write it down below.

```



```

6. **Ask yourself** *Is this fear moving me closer to my soul's calling or further away?* Note down your answer below.

```



```

7. **Lead with love.** Ask yourself *What can I tell myself that is more true and loving than my fear story?* Write that down here.

```



```

8. **Crack your courage code.** Choose one tiny thing you can do that'll move you towards your heart's desires. Note that down below – and do it!

```



```

Follow first and foremost the guidance and wisdom you receive from your soul!

EXERCISE 24: CONNECT TO YOUR INNER WARRIOR

PURPOSE:

- To recognize that you are courageous;

- To know what courage feels like for you;

- To practice your courage muscle.

INSTRUCTIONS:

1. **Think back on a time in your life when you did something that took real courage to do.** It could be anything, not necessarily what you've been told is courageous. Describe your courage story here:

2. **Find 10 examples from your life of things that took courage for you to do.** Go back to childhood and start remembering them. List them below.

   Here are a few of my courage examples that might help you to find yours:

   - *Letting go of the side of the pool in the deep end*
   - *Going alone to a new town for a summer job*
   - *Switching to psychology from biology*
   - *Buying a house by myself*

3. **Pick your most inspiring courage story and draw it below** with your nondominant hand.

```
┌─────────────────────────────────────────────────────────────────────┐
│                                                                       │
│                                                                       │
│                                                                       │
│                                                                       │
│                                                                       │
│                                                                       │
│                                                                       │
└─────────────────────────────────────────────────────────────────────┘
```

4. **Reexperience this courage story.** Remember what you did and how it felt. Feel your body sensations of courage. Describe them below:

```
┌─────────────────────────────────────────────────────────────────────┐
│                                                                       │
│                                                                       │
│                                                                       │
│                                                                       │
│                                                                       │
│                                                                       │
│                                                                       │
└─────────────────────────────────────────────────────────────────────┘
```

5. **Spend 5 minutes doing this whenever you need to find your courage.**

6. **Maintain an ongoing courage story list** by adding courage stories to your list as they happen.

EXERCISE 25: SOUL'S CALLING SUMMARY

EXPLANATION:

Now you need to integrate and make sense of all the exercises you've done. Your thinking mind can tell you that you know nothing more than when you began, but that's a lie. Never forget, your thinking mind wants you to stay in your comfort zone and not make any changes. Hearing and answering your soul's calling means that your life WILL change.

When you summarize your findings, you once more dare to decide to answer the callings of your soul. Writing all this down makes it concrete.

PURPOSE:

- To listen to your soul's calling;

- To name your "one small task".

INSTRUCTIONS:

Take 12 deep belly breaths and imagine you are rooted to the earth. Ask yourself each of the following questions and write your answers using your nondominant hand.

1. Who I am becoming?

2. What does my soul want to create?

3. What am I releasing?

4. What is my core message?

5. What are my gifts and talents?

6. What's my unique genius? Notice if this is different from your gifts and talents.

[ ]

7. What is my "one small task" in the world or my soul's purpose?

[ ]

8. What's the next step that is right in front of me?

[ ]

Make a soul commitment:

9. I commit to:

[ ]

CONCLUSION

Congratulations!

This is your life's work – to live as your soul-self in human form, experiencing both the beauty and the suffering that is present in this world.

The soul is grounded and deeply rooted in the natural world. It brings spirit to this consciousness. Some people will try to constantly move towards the spiritual plane and forget they are here on this earth for a reason. They seem unbalanced to me, intoxicated with spirituality without being grounded and present, right here, right now. Following your soul's calling is an earthly pursuit.

When you start answering your soul's calling, it doesn't mean that you'll no longer have any dissatisfaction. It doesn't mean you'll constantly be floating in a blissful state of nirvana. It means you are doing your best to live the life you were born for, living in your truth, giving love and being love as best you can.

Your soul will always guide you. Anytime you feel lost, check in and ask your soul a question. The answer will come.

The difference between how it feels at the beginning of the process, the volcano and how it feels now, when you are on the journey, is that you now have peace. The angst goes away.

In my case, I no longer worry about not knowing what I was born for. I do still worry about whether I'm doing it fully. I still navigate the unknown, get afraid and do it anyway. I have found the deep peace of living in my truth. I know my deep, inner, private place, the stillness of my own soul. I know that when I fall off track, it's just a blip, and I'll find my way back again.

I am filled with gratitude that you have come all the way through this journey. I hope the exercises, and particularly the roadmap, helped you find your way.

Don't forget: You already have everything you need. You don't need to change yourself or make yourself over. You came here with gifts to be claimed, grown and given, and that's what answering your soul's calling is all about.

Here's a final quote by Elle Luna from her fabulous book *The Crossroads of Should and Must*:

> *If you believe that you have something special inside you, and feel it's about time you gave it a shot, honor that calling in some small way – today.*

If you feel a knot in your stomach because you can see the enormous distance between your dreams and your daily reality, do one thing to tighten your grip on what you want – today.

If you've been peering down the road to must but can't quite make the choice, dig a little deeper and find out what's stopping you – today.

Because there is a recurring choice in life, and it occurs at the intersection of two roads. We arrive at this place again and again.

Dare to decide to answer the call. You won't regret it.

With so much love,

Bev.

DEFINITIONS

calling — Something you feel compelled to do regardless of fame or fortune. It uses your gifts and expresses your purpose. The work itself is the reward. A calling is not necessarily a job or a career.

career — An occupation undertaken for a significant period of time in a person's life where they advance in responsibility, competence and remuneration. You can be employed or self-employed in a career.

change — An event that happens: a move, job loss, divorce, pregnancy, etc.

ego — The part of you that is linear, methodical, past- and future-focused, designed to pick out details, and categorize and organize information. It helps you get things done efficiently. It resides in your left brain, uses language and defines you as an "I", keeping you separate and distinct from others. Ego is an artificial sense of ourselves. It is an idea, based mostly on other people's opinions that began to form when we were children. It is the person or image we've come to believe we are or think of ourselves as. This self-image is layered over our soul-self or essence-self. It makes sure you learn and incorporate the social rules of your religion, culture and peer group so you can get your survival needs of love and belonging met. Your ego is the false self you create to survive.

God (The Universe) — Same as *spirit,* defined below. Love energy that is everywhere in everything in abundance, that is waiting for you to access it.

job — Something you do for a specific number of hours a day – often 9-to-5 or 8-to-4 – for money. You are hired by someone else and are considered employed.

mission — Same as *purpose,* defined below.

one small task — A concrete representation of your genius. It is one thing you can't *not* do. It's not a job. It comes from your unique genius and answers your soul's calling. It is the thing you do to be a force for good in the world. It is the contribution you are perfectly suitable for and, no matter what it is, if you do it, it'll help the world make the transformation from ego to soul.

purpose — The answer to the question *Why are you here, on earth?*

soul — The deepest, truest part of you. An essence unique to each person, that is much deeper than personality, that is always guiding you. It is your personal connection to God and universal love energy. You feel it deep inside your heart, in the centre of your body. It is separate from your ego and communicates with you through your body and in your dreams.

Soul is a journey of descent to our earthly roots. Your soul is the true self that existed before you were born and will continue to exist after your body dies.

Soul's Calling — The emotions, felt senses and body sensations you have as your soul tries to communicate with you. This can include any emotions or feelings from joy to distress and body sensations from lightness to constriction.

soul-inspired entrepreneur — Someone who starts a business to express their calling and live their purpose. They are a new breed of entrepreneur, motivated by using their gifts to meet the world's needs, rather than being motivated by being in business. Many never dreamed they'd be in business. Making a living is important, but financial profit is a result of their work, not the goal.

spirit — The single, great and eternal mystery that permeates and animates everything in the universe and, yet, transcends all. Ultimately, each soul exists as an agent for spirit. The majestic "out there" removed from ordinary life but infused in all and everything. You connect to spirit through prayer and meditation. Spirit is a journey of ascent into the upperworld, a union with the light.

transition — The inner psychological process to adjust to a change event. This involves going through a process of endings, a period of limbo, and then a new beginning.

unique genius — The gifts and talents you were born with, including your personal style, the impact of your life experiences and what you stand for in the world. Your unique genius resides in your soul.

vocation — Same as a *calling*, defined above. Its origin is from the Latin word *vocare*, which means *to call*. This word also has religious origins and refers to a divine call to God's service.

REFERENCES

Beck, Martha. *Finding Your Own North Star: Claiming the Life You Were Meant to Live.* Harmony Press, 2001.

Beck, Martha. *Steering by Starlight: The Science and Magic of Finding Your Destiny.* Rodale Books, 2009.

Bridges, William, *Transitions: Strategies for Coping with the Difficult, Painful, and Confusing times in your life.* Addison-Wesley Publishing, Twenty-sixth printing, 1993.

Harris, Russ. *The Confidence Gap: A Guide to Overcoming Fear and Self-Doubt.* Trumpeter, 2011.

Katie, Byron. *Loving What Is: Four Questions That Can Change Your Life.* Three Rivers Press, 2003.

Luna, Elle. *The Crossroads of Should and Must: Find and Follow Your Passion.* Workman Publishing Company, 2015.

McLaren, Karla. *The Language of Emotions: What Your Feelings Are Trying to Tell You.* Sounds True, 2010.

Meade, Michael. *The Genius Myth.* Greenfire Press, 2016.

Palmer, Parker J. *Let Your Life Speak: Listening for the Voice of Vocation.* Jossey-Bass, 1999.

Romeo, Elisa. *Meet Your Soul: A Powerful Guide to Connect with Your Most Sacred Self.* Hay House, Inc., 2015.

Sher, Barbara. *I Could Do Anything If I Only Knew What It Was: How to Discover What You Really Want and How to Get It.* Delacourte Press, 1994.